You Would Be Surprised

by Susie Baretz

illustrated by Amy J. Wulfing

MAPLE LEAF CENTER, INC.
www.MapleLeafCenter.com

You Would Be Surprised
Written by Susie Baretz
Illustrations by Amy J. Wulfing
Edited by Sally-Anne Snarski

Copyright 2009 Maple Leaf Center, Inc.
167 North Main Street
Wallingford, VT 05773 USA

Digital Image © The Museum of Modern Art / Licensed by SCALA / Art Resource, NY
Gogh, Vincent van (1853-1890). The Starry Night. 1889. Oil on canvas, 29" x36 1/4".
Acquired through the Lillie P. Bliss Bequest.

Published and Distributed by

Maple Leaf Center, Inc.
167 North Main Street
Wallingford, VT 05773
Phone (802) 446-3601
www.MapleLeafCenter.com

Printed in the United States of America

ISBN: 978-0-9759850-9-0
        0-9759850-9-4
Library of Congress Control Number: 2009936252

This book is dedicated to Miles, who continues to teach me every day about love, life, and laughter; and to his very smart, funny, and highly dramatic five-year-old sister, Skylar.

You would be surprised to know
that I – yes, me – Bradley Spencer,
an eight-year-old boy with autism,
have super powers!

In fact, I was surprised when I found out
how cool everything I see, hear, taste, smell,
and feel is compared with what most people
can see, hear, taste, smell, and feel.

You would be surprised to know that
my super powers are all around me.

They are in my eyes, my ears, my mouth,
my nose, and even my fingers.

You would be surprised at the things I see.

I know most people see what they want to see and don't pay a lot of attention to the little things all around them.

Not me.

I see EVERYTHING!

I see the air and all of its dots.

Colors are so bright to me that they *almost* hurt my eyes.

Gogh, Vincent van (1853–1890).
The Starry Night. 1889.
Oil on canvas, 29" x 36 1/4".
Acquired through the Lillie P. Bliss Bequest.

I see lights dance, and I even have the power
to see beautiful pictures with my eyes closed.

You would be surprised at the things I hear.

When it seems quiet to everyone else,
it can sound *VERY NOISY* to me!

I can even hear something happening two rooms away,
like the contents of a whisper and music so soft
that many people wouldn't even hear it.

My ears hear EVERYTHING!

You would be surprised at all the things I can taste.

When I sit to eat, flavors jump up at me
from the food on my plate.

If they are yummy foods, they taste even better.

If they are yucky foods, I won't touch them!

Broccoli? What were grown-ups thinking?

You would be surprised at all the things I can smell.

This is not necessarily my favorite super power.
Maybe I won't mind it as much
when my sister stops wearing diapers. Ugh!

Good things to smell are flowers,
cookies baking, and my mom's perfume.

These smells are delightful.

You would be surprised at the way things feel to me,

like a soft furry blanket

and the bubbles in a bath.

I can be feeling pretty rotten,
and sometimes nothing but a soft fabric
can make me feel better.

The *whoosh* of air that I feel when I jump on a trampoline
can be as special to me as my favorite movie
or a piece of chocolate cake.

Oh, and I love roller coasters! Do you?
Well, they are 100 times more fun for me!
They feel faster, drop farther, and spin harder for me.
I could go around and around on them forever
without stopping!

So, are you as surprised as I was to learn about my super powers?

Before I learned how differently I see, hear, taste, smell, and feel from most people, I had no idea I had such cool super powers.

Do you have super powers too?

You Would Be Surprised is intended to celebrate a child with autism as a wonderful individual with unique abilities and perspective. Bradley's "super powers" *are* totally cool, but, they can also present many serious challenges.

Children within the autism spectrum often struggle with sensory processing. A sensory processing disorder can make it difficult for children to learn, make friends, and even feel comfortable in their own homes.

For more information and resources on Autism and Sensory Processing Disorder, please click the LINKS button on our website: **www.MapleLeafCenter.com**

About the Author

Susie Baretz

With the birth of her nephew, Miles, Susie quickly learned the meaning of immeasurable love and the beauty of life from a very unique perspective. Following Miles' diagnosis, autism became the focus of Susie's educational and professional endeavors. Currently, she resides in Chicago, Illinois, while she completes her dissertation in the field of School Psychology. In addition, Susie also leads support groups for parents of young children recently diagnosed with an Autism Spectrum Disorder.

Susie is co-creator of MagneTalk® Turns & Topics™ Magnetic Board Games for Children with Autism Spectrum Disorders. Children with Autism Spectrum Disorders (ASDs) enjoy playing games, but often "regular" game boards are too overwhelming and confusing. The simple game boards and basic Topic Cards in MagneTalk Turns & Topics are specifically for children with ASDs. The targeted games allow students to have fun and gradually increase their concentration skills while they learn basic game playing and communication skills. Please visit www.MapleLeafCenter.com for purchasing details.

About the Illustrator

Amy J. Wulfing studied illustration at The Academy of Art in San Francisco and Parson's School of Design in New York. After five years as an art director in Manhattan, she launched a solo career in character development and design. Her work has been featured on a wide range of products from wallpaper and balloons to plush animals, games, and television shows. She lives in Vermont with her wonderful husband, two amazing sons, two goofy Labs, a cat, and a "super" Bassett Hound who pretended not to mind posing in a cape.

Maple Leaf Clinic

Director, Dean J.M. Mooney, Ph.D., NCSP
167 North Main Street • Wallingford, VT 05773
Phone: (802) 446-3577 • Fax: (802) 446-3801
Email: MapleLeafClinic@vermontel.net

www.MapleLeafClinic.com

Maple Leaf Clinic, founded by Dr. Dean Mooney, provides neuropsychological, educational, psychological, speech and language, and social thinking assessments of children, adolescents and adults. Therapy for people of all ages is provided. Our services also include social skills development (utilizing Relationship Development Intervention® and the Think Social! model), educational or clinical consultation (in person, by phone, or through iChat/SKYPE), and professional development.

Maple Leaf Clinic is also proud to host Camp Maple Leaf, a summer camp that caters to the social needs and relaxation skills of campers with Nonverbal Learning Disabilities, Asperger's Syndrome, High Functioning Autism, or PDD-NOS.

Dr. Mooney is a Licensed Clinical Psychologist - Doctorate and a Licensed School Psychologist in the state of Vermont. In addition, he is a Nationally Certified School Psychologist.

He is co-author of *Nonverbal Learning Disabilities: A Guide to School Success* (May 2006), *Nonverbal Learning Disabilities: A Guide to School Success - The Teacher's Manual* (September 2007), *A Train Ride to Grandma's (With NO Chocolate Donut!)* (September 2009), and *A Snapshot of Me - A Student with NLD* (Spring 2010).

Dr. Mooney has lectured on the topic of Nonverbal Learning Disabilities for local and national organizations throughout the United States, Canada, and England. He is proud to be a member of the Health Advisory Board of the Turner Syndrome Society of the United States. Additionally, Dr. Mooney serves on the Professional Advisory Board for The College Internship Program at The Brevard Center, Melbourne, Florida, and The Berkshire Center, Lee, Massachusetts.

CAMP MAPLE LEAF

www.MapleLeafClinic.com

Camp Maple Leaf is a fun day camp experience that focuses on the development of social skills and leisure/relaxation skills for children and adolescents diagnosed with Nonverbal Learning Disabilities, Asperger's Syndrome, High-Functioning Autism, or PDD-NOS.

Philosophy

Children with Nonverbal Learning Disabilities, Asperger's Syndrome, High Functioning Autism, or PDD-NOS need a structured and nurturing environment in order to learn, practice, and master social skills. Camp Maple Leaf offers opportunities for campers to expand their social skills while having fun, learning new leisure activities, and taking social risks. This productive and supportive environment is fostered by trained peer counselors and highly qualified staff dedicated to a kind and professional learning environment.

Goals

Campers will participate in activities that will enhance appropriate social skills; be provided with opportunities to develop friendships in a carefully structured, nurturing environment; learn skills to appropriately manage sensory issues that can transfer to the home and school environment; and be given many opportunities to have fun!

Maple Leaf Center, Inc.

President, Linda J. Hudson
167 North Main Street • Wallingford, VT 05773
Phone: (802) 446-3601 • Fax: (802) 446-3801
Email: MapleLeaf@vermontel.net
www.MapleLeafCenter.com

Through our conferences, trade shows, publications, and resources, Maple Leaf Center, Inc. is dedicated to offering you the most up-to-date and accurate information about Nonverbal Learning Disabilities, Asperger's Syndrome, High Functioning Autism, and Pervasive Developmental Disorder.

Linda J. Hudson and the Maple Leaf Center, Inc. staff are proud to host conferences and attend trade shows across the United States on Nonverbal Learning Disabilities and Social Skills Training. We are your resource center for books, DVDs, toys, and learning aids relating to NLD and Social Skills Training. Whether you are an educator, a clinician, parent, diagnosed individual, or family member, we are pleased to offer you these valuable products and services.

Great Resources from Maple Leaf Center

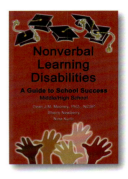

Nonverbal Learning Disabilities: A Guide to School Success

Dean J.M. Mooney, Ph.D., NCSP,
Sherry Newberry M.A., Nina Kurtz

Three professionals who work with students with NLD share their experience. Whether it is how to best present a writing assignment or how to ask a classmate to a dance, the authors have come to appreciate these students as creative, informed, and personable. Rather than focusing on the limitations of this disability, the authors believe that with a quality, comprehensive evaluation, appropriate approaches, and the input of the student, academic and social success can be achieved!

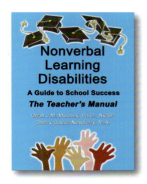

Nonverbal Learning Disabilities: A Guide to School Success The Teacher's Manual

Dean J.M. Mooney, Ph.D., NCSP, Sherry Newberry, M.A.

The ideas presented in *Nonverbal Learning Disabilities: A Guide to School Success* are brought to the point of practical application in *The Teacher's Manual*. In their previous book, developing IEP goals and instructional strategies, writing accommodations, and determining the Least Restrictive Environment, were discussed extensively. *The Teacher's Manual* provides concrete models, templates, and examples. It also includes a brief rationale and specific materials that educators can easily implement in the classroom.

The Miracle of Meghan

Sarah L. Saxton-Stevenson

A book about sharing life with a magnificent girl with Turner Syndrome

Sarah's touching memoir of her daughter's journey through Turner Syndrome is at once poignant and funny, moving and inspiring. With honesty and humor, Sarah shares her fears and tears, joys and triumphs, and offers helpful insights, practical wisdom, empathy, and strength for every parent who is raising a miracle like Meghan.

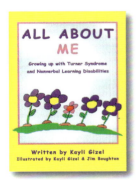

All About Me

Kayli Gizel

A heart-warming story about growing up with TS

Kayli's personal account of her experience is helpful for those seeking to understand some of the challenges that people with this syndrome, as well as NLD, face. Kayli is a delightful girl who has shown a remarkable ability to convey both personal insight and important information to the reader.

www.MapleLeafCenter.com

New Releases from Maple Leaf Center

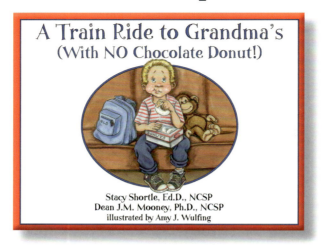

A Train Ride to Grandma's (With NO Chocolate Donut!)
Stacy Shortle, Ed.D., NCSP
Dean J.M. Mooney, Ph.D., NCSP
illustrated by Amy J. Wulfing

Noah's trip to Grandma's house is ALWAYS the same every summer. He boards the same train, sits in his favorite seat, and eagerly awaits his usual mid-trip snack while he looks out the window anticipating the usual landmarks. But, THIS year so many things are different! Noah struggles to cope with all the changes to his routine, but, in the process, he learns that sometimes doing things differently can be fun!

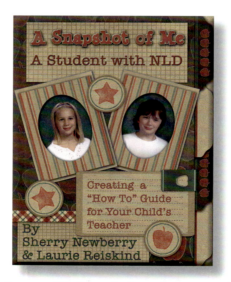

A Snapshot of Me - A Student with NLD
Sherry Newberry, M.A., Laurie Reiskind, Dean J.M. Mooney, Ph.D., NCSP

An educator teams up with the parent of a student with NLD to produce an easy "how-to" guide for creating an effective student profile. The goal of the profile is to present a clear picture of the child's history, set goals for the future, and educate teachers and professionals about NLD. This comprehensive profile follows the student with NLD throughout his or her school career.